Discovering What the Future Holds

Kay Arthur & Georg Huber

PRECEPT MINISTRIES INTERNATIONAL

WaterBroo
PRESS

D0967880

DISCOVERING WHAT THE FUTURE HOLDS
PUBLISHED BY WATERBROOK PRESS
12265 Oracle Boulevard, Suite 200
Colorado Springs, Colorado 80921

All Scripture quotations, unless otherwise indicated, are taken from the New American
Standard Bible® (NASB), © Copyright The Lockman Foundation 1960, 1962, 1963, 1968,
1971, 1972, 1973, 1975, 1977, 1995. Used by permission. (www.Lockman.org)

Italics in Scripture quotations reflect the author's added emphasis.

ISBN 978-0-307-45758-5

Published in the United States by WaterBrook Multnomah, an imprint of the Crown
Publishing Group, a division of Random House Inc., New York.

WATERBROOK and its deer colophon are registered trademarks of Random House Inc.

Printed in the United States of America
2011

10 9 8 7 6 5 4

SPECIAL SALES
Most WaterBrook Multnomah books are available at special quantity discounts when
purchased in bulk by corporations, organizations, and special-interest groups. Custom
imprinting or excerpting can also be done to fit special needs. For information, please
e-mail SpecialMarkets@WaterBrookMultnomah.com or call 1-800-603-7051.

HOW TO USE THIS STUDY

This small-group study is for people who are interested in learning for themselves more about what the Bible says on various subjects, but who have only limited time to meet together. It's ideal, for example, for a lunch group at work, an early morning men's group, a young mother's group meeting in a home, a Sunday-school class, or even family devotions. (It's also ideal for small groups that typically have longer meeting times—such as evening groups or Saturday morning groups—but want to devote only a portion of their time together to actual study, while reserving the rest for prayer, fellowship, or other activities.)

This book is designed so that all the group's participants will complete each lesson's study activities *at the same time*. Discussing your insights drawn from what God says about the subject reveals exciting, life-impacting truths.

Although it's a group study, you'll need a facilitator to lead the study and keep the discussion moving. (This person's function is *not* that of a lecturer or teacher. However, when this book is used in a Sunday-school class or similar setting, the teacher should feel free to lead more directly and to bring in other insights in addition to those provided in each week's lesson.)

If *you* are your group's facilitator, the leader, here are some helpful points for making your job easier:

- Go through the lesson and mark the text before you lead the group. This will give you increased familiarity with the material and will enable you to facilitate the group with greater ease. It may be easier for you to lead the group through the instructions for marking if you as a leader choose a specific color for each symbol you mark.

- As you lead the group, start at the beginning of the text and simply read it aloud in the order it appears in the lesson, including the Insight boxes, which appear throughout. Work through the lesson together, observing and discussing what you learn. As you read the Scripture verses, have the group say aloud the word they are marking in the text.

- The discussion questions are there simply to help you cover the material. As the class moves into the discussion, many times you will find that they will cover the questions on their own. Remember the discussion questions are there to guide the group through the topic, not to squelch discussion.

- Remember how important it is for people to verbalize their answers and discoveries. This greatly strengthens their personal understanding of each week's lesson. Try to ensure that everyone has plenty of opportunity to contribute to each week's discussions.

- Keep the discussion moving. This may mean spending more time on some parts of the study than on others. If necessary, you should feel free to spread out a lesson over more than one session. However, remember that you don't want to slow the pace too much. It's much better to leave everyone "wanting more" than to have people dropping out because of declining interest.

- If the validity or accuracy of some of the answers seems questionable, you can gently and cheerfully remind the group to stay focused on the truth of the Scriptures. Your object is to learn what the Bible says, not to engage in human philosophy. Simply stick with the Scriptures and give God the opportunity to speak. His Word *is* truth (John 17:17)!

DISCOVERING WHAT THE FUTURE HOLDS

With all that is transpiring in the world, people cannot help but wonder what the future holds. Will there ever be peace on the earth? Will the nations learn how to live in harmony with one another? Will there ever be a peaceful resolution between Israel and the Palestinians? How long will the world live under the threat of terrorism? Is a one-world ruler on the horizon?

What does the future hold for the various nations of the world? Can we know? If so, when will it happen? Where will it happen? And where do we as individuals fit into all this?

The Old Testament prophet Amos wrote, "Surely the Lord GOD does nothing unless He reveals His secret counsel to His servants the prophets" (Amos

3:7). If this is true, then God already has revealed to His people what the future holds. We've no need to worry or wonder, because He's given us a sneak preview.

Together, we're going to explore the prophecies of Daniel, which give us a clearer picture of the future than any other book of the Bible does. And as we learn, as your faith and knowledge increase, you'll find your questions replaced with trust in the One who holds the future in His hands.

If you want to construct a building that will stand firm and solid through an earthquake or any other cataclysmic event, you need to work with an experienced architect whose blueprints are followed to the letter.

God, of course, is the Architect of history and of the future, and the book of Daniel the prophet reveals His blueprints. In fact, when you understand the prophecies laid out in Daniel, you discover that every other prophecy in the Bible fits somewhere into His blueprints.

Therefore, if you want to build a solid understanding of the future and know what will happen in the "end of the days," you need to begin with the prophecies laid out in the book of Daniel.

Many people have a tendency to throw up their hands the moment Daniel is mentioned and say, "But how can a person understand this book? It's so confusing!" The problem is that many bring their own interpretations to this book, rather than allowing the interpretations given in the book to speak for themselves.

In the light of this, let's see what we can discover simply by observing the text carefully, without bringing any of our interpretations to it.

OBSERVE

Through the course of this study, we will look at each of the prophetic passages in Daniel that give insight into what will take place in the future.

Our first text is Daniel 2:25-45. Since we are breaking into the middle of the

DANIEL 2:25-30

25 Then Arioch hurriedly brought Daniel into the king's presence and spoke to him as follows: "I have found a man among the exiles

from Judah who can make the interpretation known to the king!"

26 The king said to Daniel, whose name was Belteshazzar, "Are you able to make known to me the dream which I have seen and its interpretation?"

27 Daniel answered before the king and said, "As for the mystery about which the king has inquired, neither wise men, conjurers, magicians nor diviners are able to declare it to the king.

28 "However, there is a God in heaven who reveals mysteries, and He has made known to King Nebuchadnezzar

chapter, let's first look at the context of this passage: Nebuchadnezzar, the king of Babylon, has had a disturbing dream, which none of his wise men can interpret. They say they cannot interpret the dream because they don't know what the king dreamed—and Nebuchadnezzar won't tell them. Consequently, the king is threatening to have them all put to death, including four Jewish captives who now serve Nebuchadnezzar.

When Daniel, one of the four Jewish prisoners, hears of this, he asks for time to seek counsel from the God of heaven so that God might reveal to him the dream and its interpretation. Here is where we pick up the story.

Leader: Read aloud Daniel 2:25-30. As you read, have the group...
- *draw a cloud, like this* , *around every reference to the **dream, mystery**, or **vision**.*
- *put a ? over every occurrence of the word **interpretation**.*

As you read the text, it's helpful to have the group say those key words aloud as they mark them. This way everyone will be sure they are marking every occurrence of the word, including any synonymous words or phrases.

DISCUSS

Leader: Discuss only what the group observes in the text itself. Please refrain from trying to interpret it. If people interject their thoughts, opinions, or speculations, the group will be unable to see for themselves what the pure text of Scripture reveals.

• Looking at what the group has marked, see what you can find out about the dream. Ask the "five Ws and an H"—who, what, when, where, why, and how—and see what the text tells you about the dream. For example: Who had the dream, what was it about, when did they have it, where, and why?

• If you come across any reference to time—the *when* of something—mark it by drawing a clock 🕐 over the phrase.

what will take place in the latter days. This was your dream and the visions in your mind while on your bed.

29 "As for you, O king, while on your bed your thoughts turned to what would take place in the future; and He who reveals mysteries has made known to you what will take place.

30 "But as for me, this mystery has not been revealed to me for any wisdom residing in me more than in any other living man, but for the purpose of making the interpretation known to the king, and that you may understand the thoughts of your mind."

• When you finish, have someone summarize the dream.

INSIGHT

The phrase "in the latter days" would be literally translated from the Hebrew as "end of the days." You will see this key phrase repeated as you study Daniel.

DANIEL 2:31-35

31 "You, O king, were looking and behold, there was a single great statue; that statue, which was large and of extraordinary splendor, was standing in front of you, and its appearance was awesome.

32 "The head of that statue was made of fine gold, its breast and its arms of silver, its belly and its thighs of bronze,

OBSERVE

Leader: Read aloud Daniel 2:31-35. Have the group...
> • *underline every reference to **the statue**, including the pronoun **its**.*
> • *circle every reference to **the stone**.*

DISCUSS

• What did you learn about the statue from verse 31?

• Looking particularly at verses 32 and 33, how are the different parts of the statue distinguished from one another? Mark them on the sketch below.

• What did you learn from marking the references to the statue and the stone in verses 34 and 35? Don't miss a detail.

³³ its legs of iron, its feet partly of iron and partly of clay.

³⁴ "You continued looking until a stone was cut out without hands, and it struck the statue on its feet of iron and clay and crushed them.

³⁵ "Then the iron, the clay, the bronze, the silver and the gold were crushed all at the same time and became like chaff from the summer threshing floors; and the wind carried them away so that not a trace of them was found. But the stone that struck the statue became a great mountain and filled the whole earth.

DANIEL 2:36-39

36 "This was the dream; now we will tell its interpretation before the king.

37 "You, O king, are the king of kings, to whom the God of heaven has given the kingdom, the power, the strength and the glory;

38 and wherever the sons of men dwell, or the beasts of the field, or the birds of the sky, He has given them into your hand and has caused you to rule over them all. You are the head of gold.

39 "After you there will arise another kingdom inferior to you, then another third kingdom of bronze, which will rule over all the earth."

OBSERVE

Leader: *Read Daniel 2:36-39 aloud. Have the group do the following:*

- *Mark every reference to **the king** with a box:*
- *Draw a cloud around each occurrence of **dream**.*
- *Put a ? over **interpretation**.*

DISCUSS

- What did you learn from the words you marked?

- What did you learn from marking the references to the king? Record your insights on the drawing of the statue on page 7.

OBSERVE

Leader: Read Daniel 2:40-43 aloud. Have the group...

- *mark every reference to the **fourth kingdom**, including the pronoun **it**, like this:* ⌊_____⌋
- *draw a box around every reference to the **feet** and **toes**, like this:* ⬚

DISCUSS

- What did you learn about the kingdom from verses 40-41? How is it referred to and how is it described? What part of the statue is associated with this kingdom?

- What did you learn from marking *feet* and *toes* in verses 41-43?

DANIEL 2:40-43

40 "Then there will be a fourth kingdom as strong as iron; inasmuch as iron crushes and shatters all things, so, like iron that breaks in pieces, it will crush and break all these in pieces.

41 "In that you saw the feet and toes, partly of potter's clay and partly of iron, it will be a divided kingdom; but it will have in it the toughness of iron, inasmuch as you saw the iron mixed with common clay.

42 "As the toes of the feet were partly of iron and partly of pottery, so some of the kingdom will be strong and part of it will be brittle.

43 "And in that you saw the iron mixed with common clay, they will combine with one another in the seed of men; but they will not adhere to one another, even as iron does not combine with pottery."

• What does this tell you about the fourth kingdom? What will it be like? (Don't bring in any references outside of the text; simply allow scripture to interpret scripture.) By observing the feet and toes, how many major divisions and minor divisions are given to us in this imagery? What is the relationship of the toes to one another?

DANIEL 2:44-45

44 "In the days of those kings the God of heaven will set up a kingdom which will never be destroyed, and that kingdom will not be left for another people; it will crush and put an end to all these kingdoms, but it will itself endure forever.

45 "Inasmuch as you saw that a stone was cut out of the mountain without hands

OBSERVE

Leader: Read Daniel 2:44-45 aloud. Have the group...

- *mark every reference to **time** with a clock, like this:* 🕐
- *mark every reference to **stone** with a circle:* ◯
- *mark each occurrence of **dream** with a cloud and each occurrence of **interpretation** with a question mark, as before.*

DISCUSS

• What did you learn from marking the references to time?

• When will God set up a kingdom, and what did you learn about that kingdom from these verses?

• Who are "those kings" mentioned in verse 44? Read back over verses 40-43 to get the context and flow. Once you discover who "those kings" refers to, mark the phrase accordingly.

• What did you learn from marking the references to the stone? What will happen to the other kingdoms?

• According to verses 44-45, what does the stone represent?

• Read back through the full text of the verses we've looked at, beginning with

and that it crushed the iron, the bronze, the clay, the silver and the gold, the great God has made known to the king what will take place in the future; so the dream is true and its interpretation is trustworthy."

verse 31. According to this dream, how many kingdoms will precede God's kingdom? Draw an arrow to each of them as represented on the statue below, then number them.

• When the stone sets up His kingdom, what will happen to the existing kingdom? How would knowing this help keep people from being deceived about the coming of the Lord and the establishment of His kingdom on earth?

• How accurate is the dream and its interpretation?

WRAP IT UP

Do you realize the significance of what you have just read? By considering only what the text says, what has God told you is to come? At this point, you don't want to speculate about any information not included in this passage. All you want to do is make sure you have a grasp of the facts God has given you in this prophetic dream.

God has laid out His blueprint for history, a blueprint that takes us from the Babylonian Empire of Daniel's time to the rule of God on earth—a kingdom that will never be destroyed. His kingdom will be established "in the days of those kings." What kings? The kings of the ten toes of iron and clay on two feet.

Although we might not understand it all, Scripture declares that this dream is true and its interpretation is accurate. So we know that God's kingdom cannot come on earth until there is a fourth kingdom of two divisions with ten kings, loosely aligned, some stronger than others.

If you're familiar with history, it will be obvious to you that the event described here still lies ahead, in the future. The question is, could all this take place in your lifetime? If so, would it make a difference in the way you are living—realizing that someday you will stand before the God of heaven? Wouldn't it cause you to align yourself with the Word of God even though it might not be politically correct or even seem reasonable in this day and age? Wouldn't it cause you to examine where you put your trust as circumstances change? And wouldn't it cause you to evaluate the way you spend your time and resources?

Revelation 22:12 says that when Jesus returns as King of kings and Lord of lords, His reward will be with Him to give "to every man according to what he has done" (Revelation 22:12).

What will you receive? What will He say to you?

Last week in our study of Daniel 2, we were given a broad-brush picture of the future. Like an architect's general blueprint, the vision is given with few details. However, as you turn the pages of Daniel, you come to the second segment of his book, chapters 7 through 12. In these chapters God turns our focus from the life of Daniel, a man highly esteemed by God, to visions and dreams that carefully detail not only the events that will come to pass, but also the lives and character of the major players in these events.

Our study this week will focus on Daniel 7—an incredibly exciting and enlightening chapter.

DISCUSS

Leader: Have the group review what they learned last week from Daniel 2. What was the dream about? You might want to have one of the group stand up to represent the statue and then have the group describe that statue. Have another person be the stone. Note what the stone does to the statue, where it strikes, and what happens as a result.

THE STATUE OF DANIEL 2

DANIEL 7:1-6

1 In the first year of Belshazzar king of Babylon Daniel saw a dream and visions in his mind as he lay on his bed; then he wrote the dream down and related the following summary of it.

2 Daniel said, "I was looking in my vision by night, and behold, the four winds of heaven were stirring up the great sea.

3 "And four great beasts were coming up from the sea, different from one another.

4 "The first was like a lion and had the wings of an eagle. I kept looking until its wings were plucked,

OBSERVE

Leader: Read Daniel 7:1-6 aloud. As you read the passage, have the group mark…

- *every reference to the **dream** or **vision** with a cloud as you did in Daniel 2.*
- *references to each **beast**, including synonyms and pronouns, with a half-circle like this:*

DISCUSS

- What did you learn about this dream from the opening verse? Who had it, when, where, and what was it about?

- Look at the chart on pages 104-105, which details the rulers of Daniel's time, and note when Daniel has this vision. Keep in mind that when dealing with B.C., the calendar goes from higher numbers to lower numbers as the years pass.

- What did you learn about the first beast from verse 4?

• Look at the illustrations below, and on the line provided, note which beast is the first one to appear in this dream and record what animal it resembles.

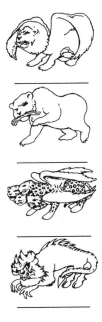

• What did you learn about the second beast from verse 5? Number and name the appropriate beast in the illustration provided.

• What did you learn about the third beast from verse 6? Take a good look at the drawing and record the kind of animal it resembles on the appropriate line.

and it was lifted up from the ground and made to stand on two feet like a man; a human mind also was given to it.

5 "And behold, another beast, a second one, resembling a bear. And it was raised up on one side, and three ribs were in its mouth between its teeth; and thus they said to it, 'Arise, devour much meat!'

6 "After this I kept looking, and behold, another one, like a leopard, which had on its back four wings of a bird; the beast also had four heads, and dominion was given to it."

DANIEL 7:7-8

7 "After this I kept looking in the night visions, and behold, a fourth beast, dreadful and terrifying and extremely strong; and it had large iron teeth. It devoured and crushed and trampled down the remainder with its feet; and it was different from all the beasts that were before it, and it had ten horns.

8 "While I was contemplating the horns, behold, another horn, a little one, came up among them, and three of the first horns were pulled out by the roots before it; and behold, this horn possessed eyes like the eyes of a man and a mouth uttering great boasts."

OBSERVE

Leader: *Now read Daniel 7:7-8 aloud.*

- *Have the group mark the reference to the **fourth beast** with a* ⌞____⌟
- *Also, have the group mark every reference to the **little horn** mentioned in verse 8, like this:* ❟

DISCUSS

- What did you learn about this beast from this verse? Make sure you don't miss any details. Also notice how it compares with the other beasts.

- How many beasts are there altogether? Have you seen that number before in Daniel? Where?

- Take a good look at the drawing of the fourth beast. Since it's not likened to a particular beast, let's name it the "D-T" (dreadful and terrifying) beast.

- What did you learn about the little horn mentioned in verse 8? What is he like? Where does he come from? When?

OBSERVE

Leader: Read Daniel 7:9-10—a continuation of the vision—aloud.

  • *Mark every reference to the **Ancient of Days,** including pronouns, with a triangle:* △

DISCUSS

• What did you learn from marking the references to the Ancient of Days?

• Who do you think this might be? Explain your answer.

DANIEL 7:9-10

9 "I kept looking until thrones were set up, and the Ancient of Days took His seat; His vesture was like white snow and the hair of His head like pure wool. His throne was ablaze with flames, its wheels were a burning fire.

10 "A river of fire was flowing and coming out from before Him; thousands upon thousands were attending Him, and myriads upon myriads were standing before Him; the court sat, and the books were opened."

DANIEL 7:11-12

11 "Then I kept looking because of the sound of the boastful words which the horn was speaking; I kept looking until the beast was slain, and its body was destroyed and given to the burning fire.

12 "As for the rest of the beasts, their dominion was taken away, but an extension of life was granted to them for an appointed period of time."

OBSERVE

Leader: Read Daniel 7:11-12 aloud and have the group mark…

- *every reference to the **fourth beast** with a ⌐___⌐ , as before.*
- *references to the other **beasts** with a half- circle:* ⌒
- *every reference to the **little horn** with a horn:* ↙
- *every reference to **time** with a clock:* 🕐

DISCUSS

- What beast is being spoken of in verse 11? How do you know?

- What happens to the rest of the beasts?

OBSERVE

Leader: Read Daniel 7:13-14 aloud, then have the group mark...

- *every reference to the **Ancient of Days**, including pronouns, with a triangle.*
- *every reference to the **One like a Son of Man** with a cross* † *(Watch the pronouns as you do this to avoid confusing them with pronouns that belong to the **Ancient of Days**.)*
- *every reference that indicates **time** with a clock:* 🕐

DISCUSS

- What did you learn about the One like a Son of Man? Don't miss any details.

- Describe the kingdom given to the One like a Son of Man.

DANIEL 7:13-14

13 "I kept looking in the night visions, and behold, with the clouds of heaven One like a Son of Man was coming, and He came up to the Ancient of Days and was presented before Him.

14 "And to Him was given dominion, glory and a kingdom, that all the peoples, nations and men of every language might serve Him. His dominion is an everlasting dominion which will not pass away; and His kingdom is one which will not be destroyed."

• Thinking back to last week's study, do you see any similarities between Nebuchadnezzar's dream and Daniel's dream? If so, what are they?

• The pictures of the two dreams are pictured below, side by side to help you compare them. Discuss only what you have observed in the text. Do not attempt to interpret Daniel 7 yet. Next week we will study the rest of the chapter, which gives the interpretation of Daniel's dream.

WRAP IT UP

Although we have not yet looked at the interpretation of Daniel's dream (which is given in Daniel 7:15-28), we have observed some exciting things this week.

Daniel received his vision in the first year of Belshazzar, king of Babylon. By this time, Nebuchadnezzar had died. And yet the dreams are quite similar, aren't they?

The statue of Nebuchadnezzar's dream had four parts, while the beasts of Daniel's dream are four in number. The fourth part of the statue and the fourth beast in each dream are given the greatest amount of attention. In Daniel 2 much attention is given to the toes of the statue, which would, of course, number ten and which are also referred to as kings. The fourth beast has ten horns on its head!

And what did you learn from the text that you just read? The horn that comes up after the ten has "eyes like the eyes of a man and a mouth uttering great boasts" (Daniel 7:8). What does that mean?

We'll wait for the interpretation next week, but let's make one last comparison for now. Did you notice that when the stone crushes the statue on the feet, then the God of heaven sets up a kingdom that will last forever? In Daniel 7, when the fourth beast is killed and the dominion of the beasts is taken away, "One like a Son of Man" is given dominion, a kingdom that will never be destroyed.

Now that ought to be very good news if you belong to God. God's kingdom is coming on earth—and "all the peoples, nations and men of every language" will serve the One like a Son of Man. This means that wherever you live, whatever your nation, whatever your language, your people will someday serve Him.

And what is the name of this One like a Son of Man? You probably know, but we will see it written in the Word, and then you will know, not because someone told you, but because you saw it for yourself in the Word of God, and His Word is truth.

By the way, if someday everyone on the face of the earth is going to serve God, don't you think this is news worth sharing, so that we can be serving Him now?

A statue of four parts crushed by a stone and four beasts whose dominion is taken away by the Ancient of Days. What is God telling us about the future? This is the question we hope to answer as we look at the interpretation of Daniel's vision of the four beasts that come out of the sea.

First Chronicles 12:32 tells us about a group of men "of the sons of Issachar, men who understood the times, with knowledge of what Israel should do." It is our prayer that this study will help you better understand the times as you discover that God has already revealed what the future holds.

May God open the eyes of your understanding as you behold wondrous truths from His Word.

OBSERVE

Leader: Read aloud Daniel 7:15-22, which appears on the following pages. Have the group…

- *put a ? over **interpretation.***
- *draw a half-circle over every reference to **beasts** in general:* ⌢
- *mark references to **time** with a clock:* 🕐

Leader: Now read through the passage again. This time have the group mark the following words with their pronouns:

DANIEL 7:15-22

15 "As for me, Daniel, my spirit was distressed within me, and the visions in my mind kept alarming me.

16 "I approached one of those who were standing by and began asking him the exact meaning of all this. So he told me and made

known to me the interpretation of these things:

17 'These great beasts, which are four in number, are four kings who will arise from the earth.

18 'But the saints of the Highest One will receive the kingdom and possess the kingdom forever, for all ages to come.'

19 "Then I desired to know the exact meaning of the fourth beast, which was different from all the others, exceedingly dreadful, with its teeth of iron and its claws of bronze, and which devoured, crushed and trampled down the remainder with its feet,

• *every reference to the **fourth beast** as before—like this:* |⎯⎯|
• *every reference to **the other horn**—the little horn—with a horn:* ↰
• *each occurrence of **saints** with a halo:* ⬯

DISCUSS

• According to verse 16, what is purpose of the verses that follow?

• What did you learn about the beasts? What is the interpretation of what they are and where they come from?

• Compare this with Daniel 7:2-3 on page 16. What then does the sea represent?

• What did you learn about the saints? What contrast is made in verses 17 and 18?

- What arouses Daniel's curiosity the most in this vision? What does he desire to know? Is there any reason why this might be his focus?

- What did you learn from these verses about the fourth beast?

- What did you learn about the little horn? Don't miss a detail.

- What did you learn about the saints?

- What did you learn from marking references to time?

- In these verses who takes predominance and for how long? What event will herald a change in power?

20 and the meaning of the ten horns that were on its head and the other horn which came up, and before which three of them fell, namely, that horn which had eyes and a mouth uttering great boasts and which was larger in appearance than its associates.

21 "I kept looking, and that horn was waging war with the saints and overpowering them

22 until the Ancient of Days came and judgment was passed in favor of the saints of the Highest One, and the time arrived when the saints took possession of the kingdom."

DANIEL 7:23-25

23 "Thus he said: 'The fourth beast will be a fourth kingdom on the earth, which will be different from all the other kingdoms and will devour the whole earth and tread it down and crush it.

24 'As for the ten horns, out of this kingdom ten kings will arise; and another will arise after them, and he will be different from the previous ones and will subdue three kings.

25 'He will speak out against the Most High and wear down the saints of the Highest One, and he will intend to make alterations in times and in

OBSERVE

Leader: Read Daniel 7:23-25 aloud. Have the group mark...

- *every reference to the **fourth beast** as before:* ⌴
- *every reference to the **little big horn** (though little, he is larger than his associates, according to verse 20) as before:* ⌣
- *every reference to the **saints** with a halo:* ⬯

DISCUSS

- What did you learn from marking the references to the fourth beast?

- Did you notice the clarifying statement about this fourth beast's kingdom, "different from all the other kingdoms" in verse 23? Put a squiggly line under it.

- What did you learn about the little big horn? Make sure you cover every detail, as this is so important.

law; and they will be given into his hand for a time, times, and half a time.' "

- What did you learn from marking *the saints*?

- Go back through the passage and mark any references to time with a clock 🕐, then read the Insight box.

INSIGHT

The phrase "time, times, and half a time" in verse 25 is another way of saying three and a half years. It is also referred to in other Scriptures as 42 months or 1,260 days. In biblical reckoning there are 360 days in a year.

DANIEL 7:26-28

26 "'But the court will sit for judgment, and his dominion will be taken away, annihilated and destroyed forever.

27 'Then the sovereignty, the dominion and the greatness of all the kingdoms under the whole heaven will be given to the people of the saints of the Highest One; His kingdom will be an everlasting kingdom, and all the dominions will serve and obey Him.'

28 "At this point the revelation ended. As for me, Daniel, my thoughts were greatly alarming me and my face grew pale, but I kept the matter to myself."

OBSERVE

Leader: *Read Daniel 7:26-28. Have the group mark...*

- *every reference to the **little big horn** and **saints,** including pronouns, as before.*
- *every reference to **the Highest One**, including pronouns, with a triangle:* △

DISCUSS

• What did you learn from marking the references to the little big horn? What happens to him and when? Compare verse 26 with Daniel 7:10 on page 19.

• What did you learn from marking *the Highest One*?

• By way of review, let's create a time line of the sequence of events leading up to the establishment of God's everlasting kingdom, based on what we've seen in Daniel 7. Begin with the first beast, which has already been noted for you, and list each kingdom that precedes the kingdom of the Highest One.

Beast #1   *Beast #2*

Lion

• According to the text, what time period immediately precedes the establishment of God's kingdom? It's the only delineated period of time given to us so far, which makes it very significant. How long will it last and what transpires during that period?

REVELATION 13:1-5

1 And the dragon stood on the sand of the seashore. Then I saw a beast coming up out of the sea, having ten horns and seven heads, and on his horns were ten diadems, and on his heads were blasphemous names.

2 And the beast which I saw was like a leopard, and his feet were like those of a bear, and his mouth like the mouth of a lion. And the dragon gave him his power and his throne and great authority.

3 I saw one of his heads as if it had been slain, and his fatal wound was healed.

OBSERVE

If we allow Scripture to speak for itself and accept God's interpretation of this dream, it should be evident that no figure in history has ever fulfilled the description of the "other horn." No one to date has risen out of a kingdom with ten kings who "devour the whole earth and tread it down and crush it" (7:23) and then is brought to an end by the coming of the Ancient of Days. Nor can we truly say that all the dominions serve and obey God, as verse 27 indicates.

Possibly you have heard about the coming of the "Antichrist," the "man of lawlessness," a one-world ruler who wreaks havoc upon the earth. The description of this end-time personality is found in Revelation 13, a chapter worth studying because of its parallels with Daniel 7.

Our final task this week will be to observe a portion of Revelation 13 that will throw light on the other horn of the fourth beast.

Leader: Read Revelation 13:1-5 aloud. Have the group...

- *mark every reference to the **beast** as they marked the fourth beast in Daniel:*

  └─────┘

- *put a pitchfork* 𝚼 *over every reference to the **dragon**.*

- *mark every reference to **time** with a clock:* 🕐

INSIGHT

In Revelation 12:9 we are given the identity of the dragon: "And the great dragon was thrown down, the serpent of old who is called the devil and Satan, who deceives the whole world."

DISCUSS

- What did you learn from marking the references to the beast?

- Do you see any similarities to events described in Daniel 7? What are they?

- What did you learn about the dragon in this passage?

And the whole earth was amazed and followed after the beast;

4 they worshiped the dragon because he gave his authority to the beast; and they worshiped the beast, saying, "Who is like the beast, and who is able to wage war with him?"

5 There was given to him a mouth speaking arrogant words and blasphemies, and authority to act for forty-two months was given to him.

REVELATION 13:6-9

6 And he opened his mouth in blasphemies against God, to blaspheme His name and His tabernacle, that is, those who dwell in heaven.

7 It was also given to him to make war with the saints and to overcome them, and authority over every tribe and people and tongue and nation was given to him.

8 All who dwell on the earth will worship him, everyone whose name has not been written from the foundation of the world in the book of life of the Lamb who has been slain.

9 If anyone has an ear, let him hear.

OBSERVE

Leader: Read Revelation 13:6-9.

> • *Once again, mark every reference to the* **beast** *and to* **the saints** *as before.*

DISCUSS

• What did you learn from marking the references to the beast?

• What did you learn from marking the references to the saints?

• Once again, do you see any similarities to what you observed in Daniel 7?

OBSERVE

Revelation 13 mentions two beasts—the one we just observed and another, often referred to as the false prophet, which we will study next. The first beast, the second beast (the false prophet), and the dragon (also known as the devil or Satan) compose an unholy trinity that plays a key role in the future.

Let's take a look at the verses in Revelation 13 that deal with the second beast—the false prophet.

Leader: Read Revelation 13:11-18 aloud and have the group mark...

- *every reference to the **second beast**, including pronouns, with a **2**.*
- *every reference to the **first beast** as you did earlier:* └────┘

REVELATION 13:11-18

11 Then I saw another beast coming up out of the earth; and he had two horns like a lamb and he spoke as a dragon.

12 He exercises all the authority of the first beast in his presence. And he makes the earth and those who dwell in it to worship the first beast, whose fatal wound was healed.

13 He performs great signs, so that he even makes fire come down out of heaven to the earth in the presence of men.

14 And he deceives those who dwell on the earth because of the signs which it was given him to perform in the presence of the

beast, telling those who dwell on the earth to make an image to the beast who had the wound of the sword and has come to life.

15 And it was given to him to give breath to the image of the beast, so that the image of the beast would even speak and cause as many as do not worship the image of the beast to be killed.

16 And he causes all, the small and the great, and the rich and the poor, and the free men and the slaves, to be given a mark on their right hand or on their forehead,

17 and he provides that no one will be able to buy or to sell, except the one who has the

INSIGHT

In Jewish mystical tradition every letter of the alphabet had a numerical equivalent, which made it possible to substitute numbers for letters and come up with a number representing a person's name.

Throughout the years, people have "added up" the names of various people in the attempt to show that a particular person was the "Antichrist"—the beast of Revelation, the little big horn of Daniel. However, while the numbers of a particular name may add up to 666, the person who becomes the fulfillment of this prophecy must fulfill everything else the Word of God says about him.

So be cautious about adding up a man's name to identify him as the Antichrist. Keep in mind that the setting, timing, and events must also line up with Scripture.

DISCUSS

• What did you learn about the second beast in verses 11-18?

Leader: The lesson actually ends at this point and you may skip ahead to read the "Wrap It Up" section. However, if you have extra group time, you may want to do the optional study that follows.

OBSERVE (Optional Section)

Although there is more to learn about the *beast* in Revelation, you can study that another time. Our task today is to understand Daniel—the "blueprint" of prophecy. Therefore let's see what Revelation says about the demise of the first beast mentioned in Revelation 13, the beast that corresponds to the fourth beast in Daniel.

Leader: Read Revelation 19:10-20 and 20:4 aloud and have the group…
   • *mark with a cross* ✝ *every synonym and pronoun that relates to the one who sits on the white horse and is called* **Faithful and True.**

mark, either the name of the beast or the number of his name.

18 Here is wisdom. Let him who has understanding calculate the number of the beast, for the number is that of a man; and his number is six hundred and sixty-six.

REVELATION 19:10-20

10 Then I fell at his feet to worship him. But he said to me, "Do not do that; I am a fellow servant of yours and your brethren who hold the testimony of Jesus; worship God. For the testimony of Jesus is the spirit of prophecy."

11 And I saw heaven opened, and behold, a

white horse, and He who sat on it is called Faithful and True, and in righteousness He judges and wages war.

12 His eyes are a flame of fire, and on His head are many diadems; and He has a name written on Him which no one knows except Himself.

13 He is clothed with a robe dipped in blood, and His name is called The Word of God.

14 And the armies which are in heaven, clothed in fine linen, white and clean, were following Him on white horses.

15 From His mouth comes a sharp sword, so that with it He may

• *mark every reference to **the beast** as before:* ⌊___⌋
• *draw a halo* ⬭ *over **anyone who does not worship the beast.***

DISCUSS

• What did you learn from marking the references to the One on the white horse?

• What did you learn about the beast in this passage?

- What did you learn about those who do not worship the beast?

- Do you see any similarities between this passage in Revelation and Daniel 7? Give the reasons for your answers.

strike down the nations, and He will rule them with a rod of iron; and He treads the wine press of the fierce wrath of God, the Almighty.

16 And on His robe and on His thigh He has a name written, "King of Kings, and Lord of Lords."

17 Then I saw an angel standing in the sun, and he cried out with a loud voice, saying to all the birds which fly in midheaven, "Come, assemble for the great supper of God,

18 so that you may eat the flesh of kings and the flesh of commanders and the flesh of mighty men and the flesh of horses and of those who sit on them and the flesh of all men, both free men and slaves, and small and great."

19 And I saw the beast and the kings of the earth and their armies assembled to make war against Him who sat on the horse and against His army.

20 And the beast was seized, and with him the false prophet who performed the signs in his presence, by which he deceived those who had received the mark of the beast and those who worshiped his image; these two were thrown alive into the lake of fire which burns with brimstone.

• Who wins? Would you be on the winning side or the losing side? How do you know?

• Compare Revelation 19:20 with Daniel 7:11: "Then I kept looking because of the sound of the boastful words which the horn was speaking; I kept looking until the beast was slain, and its body was destroyed and given to the burning fire." What do you learn from this?

REVELATION 20:4

Then I saw thrones, and they sat on them, and judgment was given to them. And I saw the souls of those who had been beheaded because of their testimony of Jesus and because of the word of God, and those who had not worshiped the beast or his image, and had not received the mark on their forehead and on their hand; and they came to life and reigned with Christ for a thousand years.

WRAP IT UP

Although what you've been learning stimulates many good questions, you need to be patient. Observe, observe, observe the text. Become thoroughly familiar with it and do not seek to interpret it through a particular system of theology. Let the Word of God speak for itself. Be patient. Not all of your questions will be answered in this study. In fact, it may raise other questions. But this is all part of the process.

Learn what you can about the Word and rest assured that in His time God will reveal His truth, precept upon precept, as you become a faithful, consistent, persistent student of His Word.

Now, let's summarize what you learned this week in Daniel 7:

• The four beasts of Daniel 7 seem to parallel the four parts of the statue of Daniel 2; however, we gain more information about them in Daniel 7. See the chart titled "Daniel: God's Blueprint for Prophecy" on page 44.

• The little big horn is part of the fourth and final earthly kingdom. He comes to power after the ten horns (kings) are established. He then assumes power, and for three and a half years he rules over all the earth and overcomes the saints of the Highest One.

• The first beast mentioned in Revelation 13 and the beast in Revelation 19–20 can be associated with the fourth beast, or little big horn, of Daniel 7 based on their similar descriptions, activity, and the time period in which they rule over the earth. The passages in Revelation give us more detail about the final days of this fourth beast and what they are like.

- At the end of the three and a half years, the little horn's dominion is taken away, and he is annihilated and destroyed forever. The beast is slain, and his body is destroyed, given to the burning fire.
- The God of heaven sets up His kingdom, which will rule over all the earth—over all people, nations, men of every language—forever. God wins!

Daniel has so much more to say that will give you further insight into what is to come. We'll look at it next week.

As you think this week on what you've learned, consider how knowing this will help you understand the times and how to live. Be like the men of Issachar (1 Chronicles 12:32).

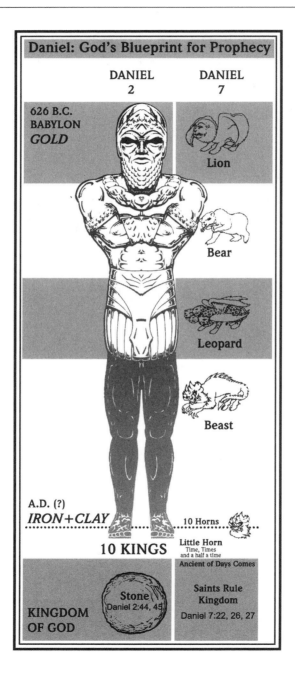

Daniel: God's Blueprint for Prophecy

DANIEL 2   DANIEL 7

626 B.C.
BABYLON
GOLD

Lion

Bear

Leopard

Beast

A.D. (?)
IRON+CLAY

10 Horns

10 KINGS

Little Horn
Time, Times
and a half a time

Ancient of Days Comes

Saints Rule
Kingdom
Daniel 7:22, 26, 27

KINGDOM
OF GOD

Stone
Daniel 2:44, 45

When you design a building, it takes a whole set of blueprints for the construction, wiring, lighting, and plumbing, each giving a separate set of details for the specific things necessary to bring the full project to completion. The prophecies in Daniel reflect a similar approach. In Daniel 2, we get the overall design of future events; then with each prophetic chapter, the specifics of those events are recorded for us in greater detail.

This week we are going to observe Daniel 8, which fills in some incredible details of God's blueprint of prophecy. It's awesome! In fact, you know it has to be divinely inspired because these prophecies were written before any of these nations were on the scene as world powers.

The first segment of the book of Daniel, chapters 1 through 6, is written chronologically and gives an account of Daniel's life not only during the reign of the Babylonians but also under Darius, king of the Medo-Persian Empire. Since our time is limited, we'll provide here a brief overview of the events in these chapters as they pertain to our study, but if you have time on your own, you'll want to read this fascinating material for yourself.

In Daniel 3, Nebuchadnezzar, the king of Babylon, builds a statue of solid gold, head to toe, and commands everyone in his kingdom to bow before it or be thrown into a furnace of fire.

In Daniel 4, Nebuchadnezzar has a prophetic dream, which Daniel interprets. The dream is a warning of what God will do so that the king and others will recognize that the Most High God "is ruler over the realm of mankind and bestows it on whomever He wishes" (verse 25). Subsequently Nebuchadnezzar loses his mind for seven years and becomes like an animal, crawling on all fours, eating the grass of the field; his hair grows like eagles' feathers, his nails like birds' claws. At the end of seven years he is restored to sanity, stands on his feet, resumes rulership of Babylon, and acknowledges the sovereignty of God. It is interesting to compare this with the description of the first beast in Daniel 7—a lion that has the wings of an eagle until they are plucked off. This beast is not only lifted up from the ground and made to stand on two feet like a man, it is also given a human mind.

In Daniel 5, another king of Babylon, Belshazzar, throws a feast to toast his gods with the holy vessels captured in the conquest of Israel. The party goes well until handwriting mysteriously appears on the wall, revealing that God's hand of judgment is about to fall. The king is slain by the Medes and Persians who, led by Cyrus, conquer Babylon.

In Daniel 6, King Darius is manipulated by jealous men who convince him to issue a decree forbidding prayer to anyone but himself for a set period of time. Daniel is thrown into the lions' den because he continues to pray to his God. God shuts the mouths of the lions, and Darius orders the deaths of those who conspired against Daniel.

Daniel 7 through 12, composing the second half of the book, record the dreams and interpretations God gave to Daniel. The visions and dreams reflect the chronology of the events in the first half of Daniel, though they were given to Daniel before those events occurred.

Now let's move on to Daniel 8, where we'll discover more about God's awesome plan.

OBSERVE

Leader: *Read Daniel 8:1-2.*

- *Have the group mark every reference to* ***the vision*** *with a cloud:*

DISCUSS

- What did you learn from these verses about the vision? Who had it, when was it given, and where was he in the vision?

- Look at the map below to see where Susa is and consult the chart "The Rulers of Daniel's Time" on pages 104-105 for further insight into the timing of this vision.

DANIEL 8:1-2

1 In the third year of the reign of Belshazzar the king a vision appeared to me, Daniel, subsequent to the one which appeared to me previously.

2 I looked in the vision, and while I was looking I was in the citadel of Susa, which is in the province of Elam; and I looked in the vision and I myself was beside the Ulai Canal.

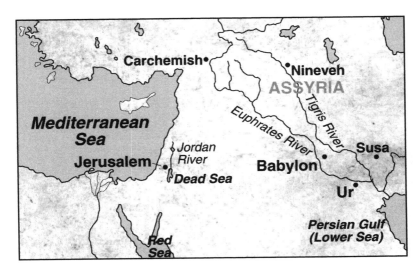

DANIEL 8:3-7

³ Then I lifted my eyes and looked, and behold, a ram which had two horns was standing in front of the canal. Now the two horns were long, but one was longer than the other, with the longer one coming up last.

⁴ I saw the ram butting westward, northward, and southward, and no other beasts could stand before him nor was there anyone to rescue from his power, but he did as he pleased and magnified himself.

⁵ While I was observing, behold, a male goat was coming from the west over the

OBSERVE

Leader: *Read Daniel 8:3-7 aloud. Have the group mark...*

- *every reference to **the ram** and its pronouns like this:* ◠◠
- *every reference to **the beasts** with a half-circle:* ◠
- *every reference to **the goat** like this:* ▬

Watch for pronouns and mark them carefully.

DISCUSS

- What did you learn about this ram? Pay careful attention to every detail; each has a purpose.

• What did you learn from marking the references to the goat?

surface of the whole earth without touching the ground; and the goat had a conspicuous horn between his eyes.

6 He came up to the ram that had the two horns, which I had seen standing in front of the canal, and rushed at him in his mighty wrath.

7 I saw him come beside the ram, and he was enraged at him; and he struck the ram and shattered his two horns, and the ram had no strength to withstand him. So he hurled him to the ground and trampled on him, and there was none to rescue the ram from his power.

DANIEL 8:8-11

8 Then the male goat magnified himself exceedingly. But as soon as he was mighty, the large horn was broken; and in its place there came up four conspicuous horns toward the four winds of heaven.

9 Out of one of them came forth a rather small horn which grew exceedingly great toward the south, toward the east, and toward the Beautiful Land.

10 It grew up to the host of heaven and caused some of the host and some of the stars to fall to the earth, and it trampled them down.

OBSERVE

Leader: Read Daniel 8:8-11 aloud and have the group...
- *put a box* ☐ *around every reference to the **rather small horn,** including the pronoun **it.***
- *mark any reference to the **Commander of the host** with a triangle:* △

INSIGHT

The word translated "host" in this passage is *tsaba* in Hebrew. In Scripture it is used to describe armies of angels, stars in heaven, and the people of God.

The references to "the place of His sanctuary" and "the holy place" are all references to the Jewish temple in Jerusalem.

Regular daily sacrifices were offered in the temple, morning and evening, according to the Law of God.

DISCUSS

• What did you learn from marking the references to the rather small horn? Where did he come from? How was he described? What did he do? Where? Don't miss any details.

• What did you learn about the Commander of the host? From the details given in verse 11, who is the Commander of the host?

OBSERVE

Leader: Read Daniel 8:11-14. We're beginning with verse 11 again for the sake of continuity. Have the group...

- *mark every reference to **the host** with a halo:* ⬭
- *mark every reference to **the regular sacrifice** with flames, like this:* ∿∿
- *underline any reference to the **place of His sanctuary** and the **holy place**.*
- *draw a box around each occurrence of **the horn,** as before.*

11 It even magnified itself to be equal with the Commander of the host; and it removed the regular sacrifice from Him, and the place of His sanctuary was thrown down.

DANIEL 8:11-14

11 It even magnified itself to be equal with the Commander of the host; and it removed the regular sacrifice from Him, and the place of His sanctuary was thrown down.

12 And on account of transgression the host will be given over to the horn along with the

regular sacrifice; and it will fling truth to the ground and perform its will and prosper.

13 Then I heard a holy one speaking, and another holy one said to that particular one who was speaking, "How long will the vision about the regular sacrifice apply, while the transgression causes horror, so as to allow both the holy place and the host to be trampled?"

14 He said to me, "For 2,300 evenings and mornings; then the holy place will be properly restored."

INSIGHT

The phrase "2,300 evenings and mornings" indicates a time span of slightly more than six years.

DISCUSS

• What did you learn from marking the references to the regular sacrifice?

• What is going to happen to the host?

• What will happen to the holy place—"the place of His sanctuary"?

• Why was the regular sacrifice removed?

• How long will these events continue?

OBSERVE

Now that we have all the details, let's see what we can learn about the interpretation of this vision.

Leader: *Read Daniel 8:15-19 aloud. Have the group mark...*

- *every reference to **the vision** with a cloud.*
- *every reference to **the time of the end** and **the final period of the indignation** with a clock:* 🕐

DISCUSS

- What did you learn from marking the references to the vision?

DANIEL 8:15-19

15 When I, Daniel, had seen the vision, I sought to understand it; and behold, standing before me was one who looked like a man.

16 And I heard the voice of a man between the banks of Ulai, and he called out and said, "Gabriel, give this man an understanding of the vision."

17 So he came near to where I was standing, and when he came I was frightened and fell on my face; but he said to me, "Son of man, understand that the vision pertains to the time of the end."

18 Now while he was talking with me, I sank into a deep sleep

with my face to the ground; but he touched me and made me stand upright.

19 He said, "Behold, I am going to let you know what will occur at the final period of the indignation, for it pertains to the appointed time of the end."

DANIEL 8:20-27

20 "The ram which you saw with the two horns represents the kings of Media and Persia.

21 "The shaggy goat represents the kingdom of Greece, and the large horn that is between his eyes is the first king.

• What did you learn from marking *time of the end* and *final period of the indignation*? According to all the preceding verses in this chapter, what would be the indignation?

OBSERVE

Leader: Read Daniel 8:20-27 aloud. Have the group do the following:

- *Mark every reference to **the ram** ᘐᘐ and to **the goat*** ✐
- *Draw a box around every reference to **the king**, beginning with verse 23 and being sure to include pronouns.*
- *Continue to mark **vision** with a cloud.*

DISCUSS

• What did you learn from marking the references to the ram and to the goat? Be sure to note each detail.

• What did you learn from marking the references to the king mentioned in verses 23-25? Note where this king comes from and when he comes to power.

22 "The broken horn and the four horns that arose in its place represent four kingdoms which will arise from his nation, although not with his power.

23 "In the latter period of their rule, when the transgressors have run their course, a king will arise, insolent and skilled in intrigue.

24 "His power will be mighty, but not by his own power, and he will destroy to an extraordinary degree and prosper and perform his will; he will destroy mighty men and the holy people.

25 "And through his shrewdness he will cause deceit to succeed by his influence; and he will magnify himself in his heart, and he will destroy many while they are at ease. He will even oppose the Prince of princes, but he will be broken without human agency.

26 "The vision of the evenings and mornings which has been told is true; but keep the vision secret, for it pertains to many days in the future."

27 Then I, Daniel, was exhausted and sick for days. Then I got up again and carried on the king's business; but I was astounded at the vision, and there was none to explain it.

• What did you learn from marking the references to the vision?

• Read the following Insight box. As you do, keep in mind that this vision was given to Daniel before Babylon was conquered by the Medo-Persian Empire. It's awesome! God is revealing to His prophet what is going to come to pass in the future!

INSIGHT

The Medes and the Persians conquered Babylon in 539 B.C., as recorded in Daniel 5. Before it happens, God reveals to Daniel the second kingdom that follows Babylon.

The Persians overpowered, then joined the Medes in 550 B.C. The Medo-Persian Empire is portrayed by the two arms of the statue in Daniel 2 and the second beast in Daniel 7. The bear raised on one side pictures the dominance of the Persians over the Medes, as does the second horn of the ram in Daniel 8, which comes up last but is larger than the other horn.

In Daniel 8, God also names the third kingdom—the bronze part of the statue which reigned "over all the earth" (Daniel 2:39)—to be Greece. This may seem unremarkable unless you realize that Greece did not become a united kingdom until Alexander the Great came to power, more than two hundred years after Daniel received the prophecy.

Because Medo-Persia was so strong, Philip of Macedonia had sought to consolidate the city-states of Greece in order to resist attack. In 336 B.C. Philip was murdered, and his son, Alexander, at the age of twenty became the first king of the Greek Empire. Within two years Alexander set out to conquer Persia. His well-trained army moved swiftly and attacked their enemy on arrival, taking them by surprise. Thus, the third kingdom prophesied by God came into power in 331 B.C.

Having no more territories to conquer, Alexander died in Babylon in 323 B.C., at the age of thirty-three, without an appointed heir. His kingdom was eventually divided among four of his generals. These are the four horns that come after the goat's first horn is broken: (1) Lysimachus took Thrace and Bithynia. (2) Cassander took Macedonia. (3) Ptolemy Soter took Egypt. (4) Seleucus Nicator took Syria.

Later from Syria, which is north of the "Beautiful Land" of Israel, came a very cruel ruler, Antiochus IV Epiphanes, who reigned from 175–163 B.C. He was the "rather small horn" who comes out of one of the four horns (Daniel 8:9) and stops the regular sacrifice, desecrates the temple in Jerusalem by sacrificing a pig on the altar, and then places a statue of Zeus in the holy place, the Holy of Holies in the temple.

Antiochus's persecution of the Jews began in 171 B.C. and ended in 165 B.C. (a span of 2,300 days, which corresponds to Daniel 8:14) when the Maccabean revolt occurred. The Maccabeans regained control of the temple in Jerusalem, removed the statue of Zeus, cleansed the temple, and reinstated the regular sacrifices. The Jewish holiday Hanukkah commemorates this event.

Antiochus IV Epiphanes died insane—"broken without human agency" (Daniel 8:25)—following military expeditions to Parthia and Armenia. Israel then ruled itself under the Hasmonean Dynasty until Jerusalem was conquered by Rome under Pompey in 63 B.C.

DISCUSS

• What information from the Insight box helps you better understand this vision of Daniel's?

• Do you think the small horn in Daniel 8 is the same as the "other horn" in Daniel 7? Explain your answer, noting where these horns came from and the situations that arose in connection with them.

• What does this vision do to Daniel, and
why do you suppose it has this affect on
him? Remember, this is *future* to him,
history to us.

• Look at the drawings of the three visions
and discuss how they correlate.

WRAP IT UP

Think about it: Before Babylon was conquered by the Medo-Persian Empire and before the Medo-Persians were conquered by Greece, God revealed it all in symbolic dreams with incredible detail. Doesn't this cause you to stand in awe!

- God makes it clear that the head of gold on the statue in Daniel 2 represents Babylon, which is detailed for us further in Daniel 7 in the description of the lion. This coincides, as mentioned earlier, with the events in Nebuchadnezzar's life recorded in Daniel 4. First, the wings of the eagle were plucked (Nebuchadnezzar's humiliation). Then the beast was lifted from the ground and made to stand on two feet like a man (Nebuchadnezzar's physical restoration). Finally, a human mind was given to it (Nebuchadnezzar's mental restoration).

- The chest of silver on the statue with two arms symbolizes the Medes and Persians, who conquered Babylon. This parallels the second beast in Daniel 7, which is raised up on one side, depicting the dominance of the Persians over the Medes. It also parallels the second horn of the ram in Daniel 8, which is longer and comes up after the first.

- The bronze follows the silver on the statue and is stronger than silver, just as the Greek Empire was stronger than the kingdom that preceded it. Greece is depicted in Daniel 7 by a leopard and in Daniel 8 by a goat, which conquers the ram, just as Greece conquered the Medo-Persian empire. The speed of the leopard with the four wings symbolizes the rapidly successful military advances of Alexander, who would quickly move his army over great distances to immediately attack enemies. The four heads on the leopard are a picture of the four generals who ascended to power after Alexander the Great died.

Although more historical detail could be added, this brief summary illustrates the awesome majesty of God's Word and again assures us that God wants His people to understand what is going to come to pass.

Remember, God does nothing that He does not first reveal to His servants the prophets. How foolish we would be to neglect the Word of God for the word of man!

As you and your friends discuss what you believe the leaders of the world ought to be doing, consider such conversations a divinely orchestrated opportunity to share what God says is going to come to pass. Meditate on the things you've been learning and ask God to show you how to help others learn what the future holds and prepare, as the book of Amos says, to meet God.

Everyone wants to know if peace will ever come to the Middle East. The answer to this question can be found in this week's study.

As we move into this next prophecy of Daniel, it's our prayer that these truths will minister to your heart and encourage you to be about the work of the kingdom, hastening the day of the coming of the Lord. May the truths provoke you to be like Daniel, a person highly esteemed by God because of his heart to know God and to understand His words.

OBSERVE

Leader: Read Daniel 9:1-3 aloud.
- *Have the group underline every reference to* ***Daniel.***

DISCUSS

- What did you learn about Daniel from 9:1-3?

DANIEL 9:1-3

1 In the first year of Darius the son of Ahasuerus, of Median descent, who was made king over the kingdom of the Chaldeans—

2 in the first year of his reign, I, Daniel, observed in the books the number of the years which was revealed as the word of the LORD to Jeremiah the prophet for the completion of the desolations of Jerusalem, namely, seventy years.

³ So I gave my attention to the Lord God to seek Him by prayer and supplications, with fasting, sackcloth and ashes.

- When did these events take place? Mark the references to time with a clock 🕐 and then look at the chart "The Rulers of Daniel's Time" on pages 104-105 so you can put the timing of this vision into its historical context.

DANIEL 9:20-23

²⁰ Now while I was speaking and praying, and confessing my sin and the sin of my people Israel, and presenting my supplication before the LORD my God in behalf of the holy mountain of my God,

²¹ while I was still speaking in prayer, then the man Gabriel, whom I had seen in the vision previously, came to me in my extreme weariness about the time of the evening offering.

OBSERVE

Leader: Read Daniel 9:20-23. Have the group...
- *underline every pronoun referring to **Daniel.***
- *circle any reference to **Gabriel.***
- *mark every occurrence of **vision** with a cloud, as before.*

DISCUSS

- What is happening to Daniel in these verses? Don't miss a thing because you learn much about him as a person.

• What do you observe about Daniel that you can apply to your own life?

• What did you learn about Gabriel?

• What did you learn about the vision?

OBSERVE

Leader: *Read Daniel 9:24-27 very slowly. Have the group…*

> • *underline every reference to **Daniel**.*
> • *mark every reference to **Daniel's people** with a halo:* ⬭
> • *mark every reference to **time** with a clock:* ⏰

22 He gave me instruction and talked with me and said, "O Daniel, I have now come forth to give you insight with understanding.

23 "At the beginning of your supplications the command was issued, and I have come to tell you, for you are highly esteemed; so give heed to the message and gain understanding of the vision."

DANIEL 9:24-27

24 "Seventy weeks have been decreed for your people and your holy city, to finish the transgression, to make an end of sin, to make atonement for iniquity, to bring in everlasting

righteousness, to seal up vision and prophecy and to anoint the most holy place.

25 "So you are to know and discern that from the issuing of a decree to restore and rebuild Jerusalem until Messiah the Prince there will be seven weeks and sixty-two weeks; it will be built again, with plaza and moat, even in times of distress.

26 "Then after the sixty-two weeks the Messiah will be cut off and have nothing, and the people of the prince who is to come will destroy the city and the sanctuary. And its end will come with a flood; even to the

DISCUSS

• Daniel 9:24-27 explains the vision the prophet was previously given. What did you learn about the vision simply from marking the references to Daniel and his people? Don't discuss anything more beyond that. We are going to observe this important passage one truth at a time.

OBSERVE

Leader: *Read Daniel 9:24 again and have the group number the list of things in the text that are to be accomplished within this specified time frame. (The first—"finish the transgression"—is numbered for you.)*

DISCUSS

• According to verse 24, what will be accomplished within this time frame?

• Among whom and where will these things be accomplished? To put it another way, to whom and to what city does this prophecy relate?

• In what period of time will these things be accomplished? Just say what the text says, then read the Insight box.

INSIGHT

The Hebrew word for "weeks" is *shabuim*, meaning "sevens." This passage offers no indication of whether the "sevens" refers to days, weeks, months, or years. The context of the passage will determine that.

• What does 70 x 7 equal? Now review what will happen in the allotted time of 70 x 7. Based on what you see, to what does 490 refer—days, weeks, months, or years?

end there will be war; desolations are determined.

27 "And he will make a firm covenant with the many for one week, but in the middle of the week he will put a stop to sacrifice and grain offering; and on the wing of abominations will come one who makes desolate, even until a complete destruction, one that is decreed, is poured out on the one who makes desolate."

• If you look at all that has to be accomplished, such as anointing the holy place—which didn't even exist at that time because the temple had been destroyed and had not yet been rebuilt—and making atonement for iniquity—which only Messiah could do—it is evident that the "sevens" are years. Therefore the things listed in verse 24 would be accomplished in 490 years.

DANIEL 9:25

"So you are to know and discern that from the issuing of a decree to restore and rebuild Jerusalem until Messiah the Prince there will be seven weeks and sixty-two weeks; it will be built again, with plaza and moat, even in times of distress."

OBSERVE

Leader: *Read Daniel 9:25, printed out here again for you.*

• *Have the group mark only **Messiah** with a cross:* †

DISCUSS

• According to Daniel 9:25, what events mark the start and finish of the time frame in question? How many weeks will occur between these two events?

• Write these two events at each end of the
line:

I———————————————————I

• Now in the middle of the line record how
much time passes between the two events.
Just put down what the text says.

INSIGHT

In 445 B.C. King Artaxerxes of Medo-
Persia issued a decree to restore and
rebuild Jerusalem. This event is
recorded in Nehemiah 1:1–2:8.

• Write the date 445 B.C. above the first
event on your time line. Now look at the
more detailed time line that follows on the
next page.

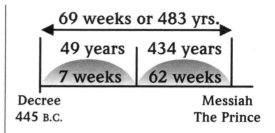

Decree
445 B.C.

Messiah
The Prince

This is a diagram of what you just observed in the text.

OBSERVE

Leader: Read Daniel 9:26 aloud, printed out here again for you. Then have the group...
- *mark any references that indicate **time** with a clock.*
- *mark **Messiah** with a cross.*

DISCUSS

- What did you learn from marking *Messiah* in 9:26?

- According to the text, when does this happen to Messiah? Draw a cross on the time line above to show where it happens in relation to the seven and sixty-two weeks.

DANIEL 9:26

"Then after the sixty-two weeks the Messiah will be cut off and have nothing, and the people of the prince who is to come will destroy the city and the sanctuary. And its end will come with a flood; even to the end there will be war; desolations are determined."

OBSERVE

Leader: Read Daniel 9:26-27 aloud once more. This time have the group...

- *mark the references to the **prince who is to come** like this:* ⌐___⌐ *(Note: Do not include "the people" in verse 26, only "the prince who is to come.")*

- *double underline **one who makes desolate**.*

- *mark any reference to **time** with a clock, as before.*

DISCUSS

- According to verse 26, who will destroy the city (Jerusalem) and the sanctuary (the temple)? Observe the text carefully.

- Discuss everything you've learned from the text about the *he* of verse 27. Then answer the question, Who is the *he* of verse 27?

- What period of time is mentioned in verse 27? According to the text, what happens in this period of time?

DANIEL 9:26-27

26 "Then after the sixty-two weeks the Messiah will be cut off and have nothing, and the people of the prince who is to come will destroy the city and the sanctuary. And its end will come with a flood; even to the end there will be war; desolations are determined.

27 "And he will make a firm covenant with the many for one week, but in the middle of the week he will put a stop to sacrifice and grain offering; and on the wing of abominations will come one who makes desolate, even until a complete destruction, one that is

decreed, is poured out on the one who makes desolate."

• How does this fit with the other sixty-nine weeks? What does this final week complete?

• Read through Daniel 9:26-27 again. According to these verses, when does "the prince who is to come" actually come? Before or after the destruction of Jerusalem mentioned in verse 26?

41 When He approached Jerusalem, He saw the city and wept over it,

42 saying, "If you had known in this day, even you, the things which make for peace! But now they have been hidden from your eyes.

OBSERVE

We learn more about this prophecy in the New Testament from Jesus Himself.

Leader: Read Luke 19:41-44 aloud.
• *Have the group underline each reference to* **the city of Jerusalem,** *including synonyms and pronouns.*

INSIGHT

In A.D. 70, the Roman general Titus besieged Jerusalem. More than one million Jews died in five months. On August 6, Roman forces invaded the temple, and just as Jesus had prophesied, not one stone was left upon another.

DISCUSS

• What did Jesus say was going to happen to Jerusalem and why?

OBSERVE

Leader: *Now read what happened in Luke 21:5-7,20-24 when Jesus was at the temple in Jerusalem. Have the group...*

• *mark every reference to the **temple** with a **T**.*

• *underline every reference to **the city of Jerusalem**.*

• *mark phrases referring to **time** with a clock:* 🕐

43 "For the days will come upon you when your enemies will throw up a barricade against you, and surround you and hem you in on every side,

44 and they will level you to the ground and your children within you, and they will not leave in you one stone upon another, because you did not recognize the time of your visitation."

LUKE 21:5-7,20-24

5 And while some were talking about the temple, that it was adorned with beautiful stones and votive gifts, He said,

6 "As for these things which you are looking at, the days will come in which there will not be left one stone upon another which will not be torn down."

7 They questioned Him, saying, "Teacher, when therefore will these things happen? And what will be the sign when these things are about to take place?"

20 "But when you see Jerusalem surrounded by armies, then recognize that her desolation is near.

21 "Then those who are in Judea must flee to the mountains, and those who are in the midst of the city must leave, and those who are in the country must not enter the city;

DISCUSS

• What did you learn about the temple from these verses?

• From what you observed in these passages, what will happen to Jerusalem and what are the people going to do?

• What will happen to the people? According to verse 24, where will they go? How long will Jerusalem be trampled underfoot?

INSIGHT

"The times of the Gentiles" seems to relate to "the fullness of the Gentiles" in Romans 11:25-26, in which Paul wrote that a partial hardening to the gospel had happened to Israel *until* the fullness of the Gentiles comes in: "And so all Israel will be saved; just as it is written, 'The Deliverer will come from Zion, He will remove ungodliness from Jacob.'"

From these two passages, the times of the Gentiles appears to be when God is dealing with Gentile nations, bringing some Gentiles to salvation. When the last Gentiles come to faith (in other words, when the fullness of the Gentiles has come), then God will bring the remnant of Israel to salvation with the coming of the Messiah, Jesus Christ, to set up His kingdom.

22 because these are days of vengeance, so that all things which are written will be fulfilled.

23 "Woe to those who are pregnant and to those who are nursing babies in those days; for there will be great distress upon the land and wrath to this people;

24 and they will fall by the edge of the sword, and will be led captive into all the nations; and Jerusalem will be trampled under foot by the Gentiles until the times of the Gentiles are fulfilled."

DANIEL 9:26-27

26 "Then after the sixty-two weeks the Messiah will be cut off and have nothing, and the people of the prince who is to come will destroy the city and the sanctuary. And its end will come with a flood; even to the end there will be war; desolations are determined.

27 "And he will make a firm covenant with the many for one week, but in the middle of the week he will put a stop to sacrifice and grain offering; and

OBSERVE

Now let's return to Daniel 9 and figure out the sequence of events according to Daniel 9:26-27.

Leader: Read Daniel 9:26-27 one more time. Have the group mark…
- *all of the phrases referring to **time** with a clock.*
- *every reference to **the prince who is to come** with a* ⌞____⌟

DISCUSS

- Take a look at the time line below. Write A.D. 70 to show when Jerusalem and the sanctuary, or temple, are destroyed. (Note who destroys the city and the sanctuary: the *people* of the prince to come.)

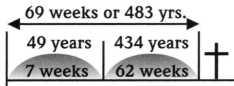

69 weeks or 483 yrs.

49 years | 434 years

7 weeks | 62 weeks

Decree
445 B.C.

• What does the "prince who is to come" do with "the many" (referring to the Jews)? Remember, this concerns Israel, Daniel's people.

• For how many "weeks," or years, will this continue?

• Then what happens?

• Where does this final seven years (the seventieth week) fit on the chart on page 76? Write it in.

• According to 9:27, how are the final seven years—the seventieth week—divided? Write this on the chart as well.

• What would have to be in place for Jews to observe sacrifices and grain offerings? Then what must be rebuilt before the seven years begin?

on the wing of abominations will come one who makes desolate, even until a complete destruction, one that is decreed, is poured out on the one who makes desolate."

• Is there a Jewish temple in Jerusalem on the Temple Mount now? Is there talk of building one? What is on the Temple Mount now?

• If they started rebuilding the temple, what would that tell you?

• What did you learn from verse 27 about the one who comes "on the wing of abominations"?

Let's look again at the time line for Daniel 9:24-27.

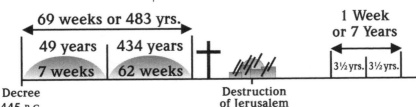

• What happens between the sixty-ninth
and seventieth weeks? Or to put it another way—after the 483 years but before the
last 7 that bring the total to 490 years?

• There's an interruption in the seventy
weeks, isn't there? Could that unaccount-
ed time possibly be the "times of the Gentiles"? If so, to what part of the statue in
Daniel 2 would it correspond? Think
about it. The Roman Empire was divided,
like two legs, into eastern and western
empires. However, it was never divided
into ten kings (the ten toes, the ten horns)
with another king (horn) coming to
power and ruling over the whole earth for
three and a half years.

Leader: *If you don't have time, the group can
read and think over the "Wrap It Up" section
on their own. This is heavy stuff, and it does
take some thinking!*

WRAP IT UP

Daniel 9:24-27 reveals what is probably the most incredible prophecy in the book, as it lays out the time line for the coming of the Messiah—not only His first coming as the sacrifice for the sins of humanity but also His second coming as the reigning King.

It tells us that Messiah the Prince will arrive 483 years after the decree to restore and rebuild Jerusalem. Just before His crucifixion, Jesus came riding into Jerusalem on a donkey, being hailed as "the King who comes in the name of the LORD" (Luke 19:38). The first sixty-nine weeks of Daniel's seventy were fulfilled.

Right after this, Jesus wept for Jerusalem because the people did not recognize the time of their visitation.

Days after this, Messiah was "cut off"—Jesus was crucified. The times of the Gentiles had begun. Jesus was going to save both Jews and Gentiles and bring them into His body, the church. The mystery of the church was now revealed through the apostle Paul (Ephesians 2–3).

As you and I are faithful to proclaim the gospel, we are hastening the second coming of the Son of God. For when that last sheep is brought into the fold, then the seals of the scroll in the hand of God (Revelation 5–6) will be broken by the Son of Man, and the last seven years of Daniel's seventy weeks will begin.

The temple will have been rebuilt in Jerusalem, the sacrifices will have been reinstated, and all will seem well for Israel. There will be peace in the Middle East.

The eleventh horn in Daniel 7:24, which corresponds to the king, the eighth beast that "was, and is not, and is about to come up out of the abyss" (Revelation 17:8,11)—that revived Roman Empire with its eastern and western divisions—will come to power, its leader making a seven-year covenant with "the many" Jews. However, when the prince breaks the covenant after three and a half years, he, like his predecessor, Antiochus IV Epiphanes, will bring desolation upon Israel. This will last for three and a half years more. Then Messiah will come, and the Ancient of Days will establish His kingdom, which will never be destroyed. And "the greatness of all the kingdoms under the whole heaven will be given to the people of the saints of the Highest One; His kingdom will be an everlasting kingdom, and all the dominions will serve and obey Him" (Daniel 7:27).

We'll look at this next week.

The question that needs to be asked today and answered by you is this: What will you do until you see the Lord face to face? Will you be faithful to God, to His Word? Will you be occupied with your business or His?

O Beloved, look at what is happening in the world. Look at what is happening in Israel. Don't miss the "time of your visitation." Think on these truths and "be steadfast, immovable, always abounding in the work of the Lord, knowing that your toil is not in vain in the Lord" (1 Corinthians 15:58). Jesus is coming again, and His reward is with Him, to give to everyone according to what he or she has done (Revelation 22:12).

Let's be about His business!

Let's look at God's final blueprint of prophecy in the book of Daniel. You'll find this so exciting, as we literally get a preview of the end of time!

Daniel 10–12 covers the final vision given to Daniel. Obviously we don't have time in a six-week, forty-minute study to cover these chapters verse by verse. However, we will cover those verses that relate to the final part of the prophecy that hasn't yet been fulfilled. These passages detail to a greater extent what will take place before God establishes His kingdom on the earth. Who knows—with the way events are transpiring, it could happen far more quickly than we think!

OBSERVE

Leader: Read Daniel 10:1-3, 10-12, and 14 aloud. Have the group do the following:

- *Put a cloud around every reference to the **vision** and **message.***
- *Mark every reference to **time** with a clock:* 🕐
- *Underline every reference to **Daniel**, including pronouns.*

DISCUSS

- What did you learn from marking *Daniel*? Answer as many of the "five Ws and an H" questions as you can about him from the text. As you look at these

DANIEL 10:1-3, 10-12, 14

1 In the third year of Cyrus king of Persia a message was revealed to Daniel, who was named Belteshazzar; and the message was true and one of great conflict, but he understood the message and had an understanding of the vision.

2 In those days, I, Daniel, had been mourning for three entire weeks.

3 I did not eat any tasty food, nor did meat or wine enter my mouth, nor did I use any ointment at all until the entire three weeks were completed.

10 Then behold, a hand touched me and set me trembling on my hands and knees.

11 He said to me, "O Daniel, man of high esteem, understand the words that I am about to tell you and stand upright, for I have now been sent to you." And when he had spoken this word to me, I stood up trembling.

12 Then he said to me, "Do not be afraid, Daniel, for from the first day that you set your heart on

references, you'll get a good sense of this man's character and faithfulness. This is a man God says is "of high esteem" (literally "preciousness"—a term that was not uniquely feminine in those days).

• Look at the chart "The Rulers of Daniel's Time" on pages 104-105 and note when Daniel receives this vision.

• What did you learn about the vision? To whom does it pertain and when is it to be fulfilled?

OBSERVE

As was pointed out earlier, chapters 10, 11, and 12 of Daniel all pertain to the vision given Daniel in the third year of Cyrus, king of Persia. The first part of this vision is recorded in Daniel 11:1-35. The prophecies were fulfilled with incredible accuracy during the reign of the last four kings of the Medo-Persian Empire and then in the reign of Alexander the Great, the one-horned goat whose horn was broken and replaced with four horns.

The Greek Empire was divided among four of Alexander's generals twenty-two years after his death. However, only two of these dynasties played a major role in the history of Daniel's people, the Jews. In Daniel 11:5-19, the two dynasties are referred to as the kings of the South (Egypt) and the kings of the North (Syria). In Daniel 11:21-35, we come to the prophecy fulfilled in Antiochus IV Epiphanes, the king of the North (Syria).

All of this information is included in the chart "History of Israel's Relationship to the Kings of Daniel 11" on page 103. This is for your personal information if you care to look at it on your own.

While all of the events of Daniel 11:1-35 were yet future for Daniel and his people, they are now history for us. The portion of Daniel that remains yet to be fulfilled with the same accuracy is Daniel 11:36–12:13. This is what we want to look at next.

Since Daniel 11:35 lets us know that the "end time" has not yet come, we will begin there.

understanding this and on humbling yourself before your God, your words were heard, and I have come in response to your words.

14 "Now I have come to give you an understanding of what will happen to your people in the latter days, for the vision pertains to the days yet future."

DANIEL 11:35-39

35 "Some of those who have insight will fall, in order to refine, purge, and make them pure until the end time; because it is still to come at the appointed time.

36 "Then the king will do as he pleases, and he will exalt and magnify himself above every god and will speak monstrous things against the God of gods; and he will prosper until the indignation is finished, for that which is decreed will be done.

37 "He will show no regard for the gods of his fathers or for the desire of women, nor will he show regard for

Leader: Read Daniel 11:35-39. Have the group...

- *mark every reference to **the king,** first mentioned in 11:36, just as you did the fourth beast: |____| Be sure to include any pronouns.*
- *mark every reference to **time** with a clock, then underline the phrase connected with that time.*

DISCUSS

- What did you learn from marking the references to the king?

- What did you learn from marking the references to time? For how long will the king prosper?

• Daniel 11:36 says that which "is decreed will be done." In the reference to the one who comes on the wing of abominations and makes desolate in Daniel 9:27, the text also says a "complete destruction, one that is decreed" will be poured out on the one who makes desolate. "Makes desolate" can be translated "causes horror." Could this king be the horn of Daniel 7 who comes up among the ten horns, pulls out three of those horns, and then rules the world? Could he be "the prince" mentioned in Daniel 9, whose appearance marks the start of the final seven years?

any other god; for he will magnify himself above them all.

38 "But instead he will honor a god of fortresses, a god whom his fathers did not know; he will honor him with gold, silver, costly stones and treasures.

39 "He will take action against the strongest of fortresses with the help of a foreign god; he will give great honor to those who acknowledge him and will cause them to rule over the many, and will parcel out land for a price."

DANIEL 11:40-45

40 "At the end time the king of the South will collide with him, and the king of the North will storm against him with chariots, with horsemen and with many ships; and he will enter countries, overflow them and pass through.

41 "He will also enter the Beautiful Land, and many countries will fall; but these will be rescued out of his hand: Edom, Moab and the foremost of the sons of Ammon.

42 "Then he will stretch out his hand against other countries, and the land of Egypt will not escape.

OBSERVE

Leader: Read Daniel 11:40-45. Have the group...

- *mark every reference to the **king** (including pronouns), as you have been doing:* ⌐_____⌐
- *mark every reference to **time**, with a clock, as before.*
- *double underline all **geographical locations**.*

INSIGHT

This prophecy pertains to Daniel's people, the Jews. The "Beautiful Land" is the land of Israel. The phrase "between the seas and the beautiful Holy Mountain" in verse 45 refers to the Mediterranean Sea and the Dead Sea and the Temple Mount in Jerusalem.

DISCUSS

- What did you learn from marking the references to the king?

• When are these events going to take place?

• Discuss what will happen to the king, according to verse 45.

• How does this prophecy fit with Daniel 7:11: "Then I kept looking because of the sound of the boastful words which the horn was speaking; I kept looking until the beast was slain, and its body was destroyed and given to the burning fire"?

• How does it fit with Daniel 9:27: "And on the wing of abominations will come one who makes desolate, even until a complete destruction, one that is decreed, is poured out on the one who makes desolate"?

43 "But he will gain control over the hidden treasures of gold and silver and over all the precious things of Egypt; and Libyans and Ethiopians will follow at his heels.

44 "But rumors from the East and from the North will disturb him, and he will go forth with great wrath to destroy and annihilate many.

45 "He will pitch the tents of his royal pavilion between the seas and the beautiful Holy Mountain; yet he will come to his end, and no one will help him."

DANIEL 11:45–12:1

45 "He will pitch the tents of his royal pavilion between the seas and the beautiful Holy Mountain; yet he will come to his end, and no one will help him.

12:1 "Now at that time Michael, the great prince who stands guard over the sons of your people, will arise. And there will be a time of distress such as never occurred since there was a nation until that time; and at that time your people, everyone who is found written in the book, will be rescued."

OBSERVE

Leader: Read Daniel 11:45–12:1 aloud. We will read the last verse of chapter 11 so that you can observe the flow of thought leading into chapter 12. Remember the Bible was not written with verse and chapter divisions; those were added later. Have the group do the following:

- *Mark every reference to **time.***
- *Draw a box around **time of distress.***
- *Put a halo over every reference to **Daniel's people.***

DISCUSS

- What did you learn from marking *the time of distress?*

- What will happen to Daniel's people during this time?

- Think back to what we studied in Daniel 7 and Daniel 9. Are there other references in Daniel that indicate his people, the Jews, will encounter distress?

OBSERVE

Three other places in Scripture refer to this time of distress "such as never occurred since there was a nation until that time": Joel 2:1-2; Matthew 24:21; and Mark 13:19. (The last two both quote the same comments from Christ.)

Leader: *Read Joel 2:1-2. Have the group...*
- *circle* **there has never been anything like it.**
- *double underline all* **geographical locations.**

DISCUSS

- What did you learn from Joel about this time of distress? How is this time described?

- To whom is God speaking in this passage? Look at the geographical locations.

JOEL 2:1-2

¹ Blow a trumpet in Zion, and sound an alarm on My holy mountain! Let all the inhabitants of the land tremble, for the day of the LORD is coming; surely it is near,

² a day of darkness and gloom, a day of clouds and thick darkness. As the dawn is spread over the mountains, so there is a great and mighty people; there has never been anything like it, nor will there be again after it to the years of many generations.

MATTHEW 24:15-21

[Jesus is speaking to His Jewish disciples in this passage.]

15 "Therefore when you see the abomination of desolation which was spoken of through Daniel the prophet, standing in the holy place (let the reader understand),

16 then those who are in Judea must flee to the mountains;

17 "Whoever is on the housetop must not go down to get the things out that are in his house.

18 "Whoever is in the field must not turn back to get his cloak.

OBSERVE

Leader: Read Matthew 24:15-21 aloud. Have the group...

- *circle* **such as has not occurred since the beginning of the world.**
- *double underline all* **geographical locations.**
- *mark every reference to* **time** *or to* **sequences of time** *such as "when" or "then" with a clock:* ⏰
- *draw a line connecting all the clocks you marked.*

DISCUSS

- What did you learn from Matthew about this time of distress? How is this time described?

- What did you learn from marking the geographical locations?

- Look at the instructions carefully. To whom are these instructions being given? How do you know?

- What did you learn from connecting the clocks about when the "great tribulation" will come?

19 "But woe to those who are pregnant and to those who are nursing babies in those days!

20 "But pray that your flight will not be in the winter, or on a Sabbath.

21 "For then there will be a great tribulation, such as has not occurred since the beginning of the world until now, nor ever will."

DANIEL 12:4-13

⁴ "But as for you, Daniel, conceal these words and seal up the book until the end of time; many will go back and forth, and knowledge will increase."

⁵ Then I, Daniel, looked and behold, two others were standing, one on this bank of the river and the other on that bank of the river.

⁶ And one said to the man dressed in linen, who was above the waters of the river, "How long will it be until the end of these wonders?"

⁷ I heard the man dressed in linen, who was above the waters

OBSERVE

Now let's go back to Daniel 12 and see what happens next.

Leader: Read Daniel 12:4-13. Have the group...

- *mark every reference to **time**, including the phrases **the end** or **the end time** with a clock:* 🕐
- *put a halo* ⬭ *over any reference to **Daniel's holy people.***
- *circle **regular sacrifice** and **abomination of desolation.***

DISCUSS

- Look at verses 4 and 9. For how long will this book and its visions be sealed up?

- According to verses 6-7, what will be the end of these wonders? Notice what has to happen to Daniel's holy people first.

(*Saints* is another word for holy.) Then what will happen? What time frame is involved here?

• What comparison can you make between what is described here and Daniel 7:25: "He will speak out against the Most High and wear down the saints [literally, *the holy ones*] of the Highest One, and he will intend to make alterations in times and in law; and they [the holy ones] will be given into his hand for a time, times, and half a time"?

• How long will it be from the abolishing of the regular sacrifice and the setting up of the abomination of desolation until this events described come to a conclusion? (Look at verse 11.)

of the river, as he raised his right hand and his left toward heaven, and swore by Him who lives forever that it would be for a time, times, and half a time; and as soon as they finish shattering the power of the holy people, all these events will be completed.

8 As for me, I heard but could not understand; so I said, "My lord, what will be the outcome of these events?"

9 He said, "Go your way, Daniel, for these words are concealed and sealed up until the end time.

10 "Many will be purged, purified and refined, but the

wicked will act wickedly; and none of the wicked will understand, but those who have insight will understand.

11 "From the time that the regular sacrifice is abolished and the abomination of desolation is set up, there will be 1,290 days.

12 "How blessed is he who keeps waiting and attains to the 1,335 days!

13 "But as for you, go your way to the end; then you will enter into rest and rise again for your allotted portion at the end of the age."

• Do you see any parallels between these verses in Daniel 12 and Daniel 9:27, which says, "And he will make a firm covenant with the many for one week [seven years], but in the middle of the week [after three and a half years] he will put a stop to sacrifice and grain offering [these are the regular sacrifices]; and on the wing of abominations will come one who makes desolate, even until a complete destruction, one that is decreed, is poured out on the one who makes desolate"?

• What parallels do you observe between the actions of the little big horn of Daniel 7 and the "abomination of desolation" in Daniel 12?

You already read about the abomination of desolation in Daniel 12 and in Matthew

24:15, which references Daniel. Remember how Antiochus IV Epiphanes put a statue of Zeus in the holy place and desecrated the temple? Second Thessalonians 2:3-4 tells us that when the man of lawlessness is revealed—"the son of destruction, who opposes and exalts himself above every so-called god or object of worship"—he will take "his seat in the temple of God, displaying himself as being God." This is:

(1) the abomination of desolation referred to in Daniel 12;

(2) the action of the little big horn of Daniel 7 who devours the whole earth, treads it down and crushes it; and

(3) the prince who breaks the covenant, stops the regular sacrifices, and makes desolate as mentioned in Daniel 9.

• What does the text reveal about the 1,290 and 1,335 days? What does this mean?

Leader: *Read the Insight box aloud.*

INSIGHT

Some believe that the extra thirty days referred to in verse 11 (beyond the 1,260 days, or three and a half years) may have to do with events surrounding the coming of the Ancient of Days and the establishment of His kingdom. We really don't know for sure.

Nor do we know for sure what the blessing is for those who wait and attain to the 1,335 days. It may be that these are faithful ones who persevere through the judgment of the nations and the separation of the sheep from the goats, spoken of in Matthew 25.

Leader: *If time allows, you may want to review the chart "Prophetic Overview of Daniel" on the next page. Otherwise move ahead to the next discussion questions.*

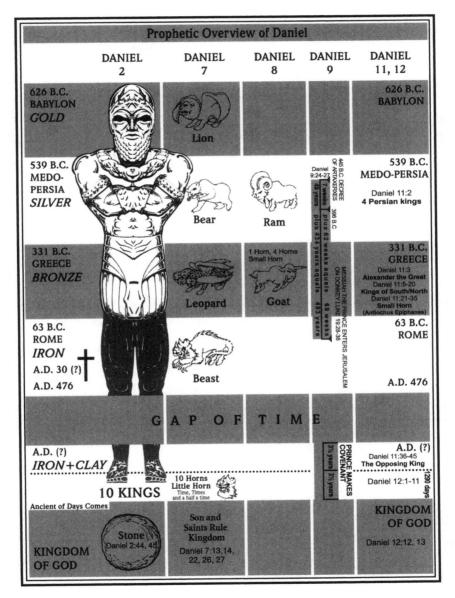

Reprinted with permission from the *New Inductive Study Bible*

DISCUSS

• If the head of gold on the statue was Babylon, and the Medes and the Persians followed Babylon, and if the Greek Empire followed the Medo-Persian Empire, what empire came next? Who conquered Greece? What empire is the fourth kingdom?

• History tells us that Rome conquered Greece. Why is the fourth beast—the dreadful and terrifying beast, the Roman Empire—different from the others? Is it because this kingdom existed right through the time of Christ until it eventually divided—like the two legs—into eastern and western empires, until both came to an end? Yet it had neither ten divisions nor a horn that came up after the ten, did it?

• We know from God's Word that there is no other kingdom. The fourth is the last, the one in which God sets up His own kingdom in the days of the ten horns and the little big horn that rules the world. Could the fourth beast, dreadful and terrifying, signify a kingdom that ends but eventually returns, trampling the whole earth and overpowering God's holy people for three and a half years? Will the ten toes be ten different kingdoms or the world divided into ten different regions? Time will tell—while you watch with interest and insight as it comes to pass.

Through the study of the past six weeks, you've been equipped to understand what the future holds. Watch what happens when people are weary of wars and rumors of wars and want a world ruler who promises peace.

When that happens, look up, for your redemption draws near.

WRAP IT UP

We've covered so much ground—how do we wrap all this up? We examine how we are going to live in the light of it all. We are to be like those described in Daniel 12:3; we are to shine brightly in this dark world and lead many to righteousness, because Jesus is coming and His reward is with Him to give to each of us according to our deeds.

Don't forget Daniel 11:32-33: " 'But the people who know their God will display strength and take action. Those who have insight among the people will give understanding to the many.' "

Listen and hear the words of 2 Peter 3:10-15:

> But the day of the Lord will come like a thief, in which the heavens will pass away with a roar and the elements will be destroyed with intense heat, and the earth and its works will be burned up. Since all these things are to be destroyed in this way, what sort of people ought you to be in holy conduct and godliness, looking for and hastening the coming of the day of God, because of which the heavens will be destroyed by burning, and the elements will melt with intense heat!
>
> But according to His promise we are looking for new heavens and a new earth, in which righteousness dwells.
>
> Therefore, beloved, since you look for these things, be diligent to be found by Him in peace, spotless and blameless, and regard the patience of our Lord as salvation.

History of Israel's Relationship to the Kings of Daniel 11

Alexander the Great
336-323 B.C.

The Large Horn of the Shaggy Goat of Greece (8:21)

Twenty-two years after Alexander's death, Greece was divided among four of his generals (8:22):

Lysimachus	Cassander	Ptolemy I Soter	Seleucus I Nicator
took Thrace and Bithynia	took Macedonia	took Egypt	took Syria

Only Ptolemy I Soter and Seleucus I Nicator relate to Israel.

Kings of the North—Syria

1. Seleucus I Nicator, 312-281 B.C. (11:5)
2. Antiochus I Soter (not referred to in Daniel)
3. Antiochus II Theos, 262-246 B.C. (11:6)
4. Seleucus II Callinicus, 246-226 B.C. (11:7-9)
5. Seleucus III Ceraunus, 226-223 B.C. (11:10)
*6. Antiochus III the Great, 223-187 B.C. (11:10, 11, 13, 15-19)
*7. Seleucus IV Philopator, 187-175 B.C. (11:20)
*8. Antiochus IV Epiphanes, 175-163 B.C. (11:21-35)
(younger son of Antiochus III the Great)

Kings of the South—Egypt

*1. Ptolemy I Soter, 323-285 B.C. (11:5)

*2. Ptolemy II Philadelphus, 285-245 B.C. (11:6) ————— Marriage

*3. Ptolemy III Euergetes, 245-221 B.C. (11:7-9) ————— 2 Wars

*4. Ptolemy IV Philopator, 221-203 B.C. (11:11, 12) ————— 2 Wars

*5. Ptolemy V Epiphanes, 203-181 B.C. (11:14, 15, 17) ————— War/Marriage

6. Ptolemy VI Philometor, 181-145 B.C. (11:25)

* These kings ruled Israel

Reprinted with permission from the *New Inductive Study Bible*

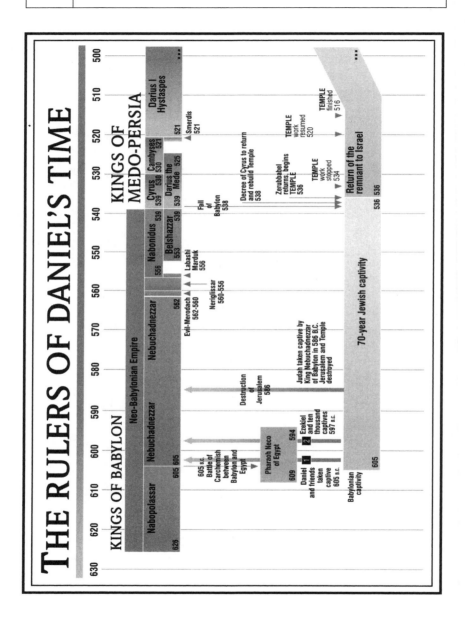

THE RULERS OF DANIEL'S TIME

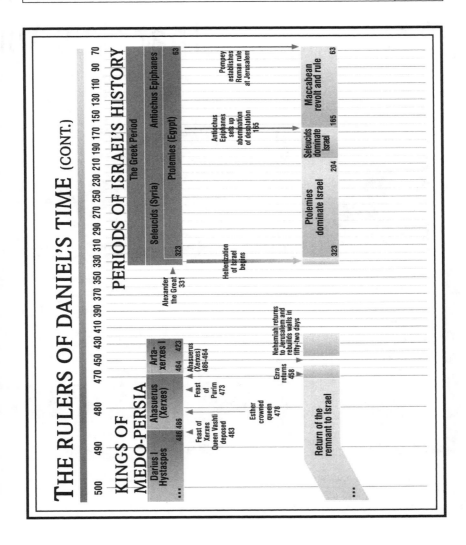

THE RULERS OF DANIEL'S TIME (CONT.)

PERIODS OF ISRAEL'S HISTORY

500 490 480 470 450 430 410 390 370 350 330 310 290 270 250 230 210 190 170 150 130 110 90 70

KINGS OF MEDO-PERSIA

Darius I Hystaspes
...
486 486

Ahasuerus (Xerxes)

Arta-xerxes I
464 423

Ahasuerus (Xerxes) 486-464

Feast of Xerxes Queen Vashti deposed 483

Esther crowned queen 478

Feast of Purim 473

Ezra returns 458

Nehemiah returns to Jerusalem and rebuilds walls in fifty-two days

Return of the remnant to Israel
...

The Greek Period

Seleucids (Syria)

Antiochus Epiphanes

Ptolemies (Egypt)
323 63

Alexander the Great 331

Hellenization of Israel begins

Antiochus Epiphanes sets up abomination of desolation 165

Pompey establishes Roman rule at Jerusalem

Ptolemies dominate Israel
323 204

Seleucids dominate Israel
165

Maccabean revolt and rule
63

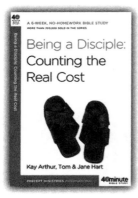
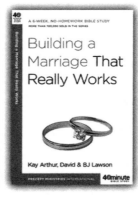
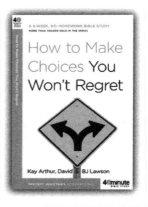

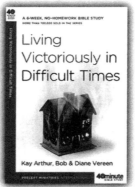

Bible Studies
Discover Truth For Yourself

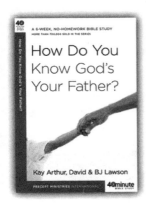

A 6-WEEK, NO-HOMEWORK BIBLE STUDY
MORE THAN 700,000 SOLD IN THE SERIES

How Do You Know God's Your Father?

Kay Arthur, David & BJ Lawson

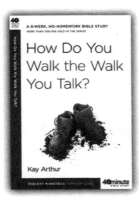

A 6-WEEK, NO-HOMEWORK BIBLE STUDY
MORE THAN 700,000 SOLD IN THE SERIES

How Do You Walk the Walk You Talk?

Kay Arthur

A 6-WEEK, NO-HOMEWORK BIBLE STUDY
MORE THAN 700,000 SOLD IN THE SERIES

Money and Possessions: The Quest for Contentment

Kay Arthur & David Arthur

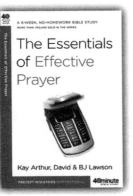

A 6-WEEK, NO-HOMEWORK BIBLE STUDY
MORE THAN 700,000 SOLD IN THE SERIES

The Essentials of Effective Prayer

Kay Arthur, David & BJ Lawson

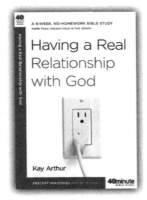

A 6-WEEK, NO-HOMEWORK BIBLE STUDY
MORE THAN 700,000 SOLD IN THE SERIES

Having a Real Relationship with God

Kay Arthur

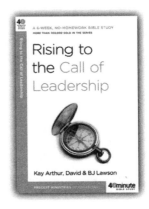

A 6-WEEK, NO-HOMEWORK BIBLE STUDY
MORE THAN 700,000 SOLD IN THE SERIES

Rising to the Call of Leadership

Kay Arthur, David & BJ Lawson

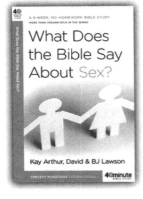

A 6-WEEK, NO-HOMEWORK BIBLE STUDY
MORE THAN 700,000 SOLD IN THE SERIES

What Does the Bible Say About Sex?

Kay Arthur, David & BJ Lawson

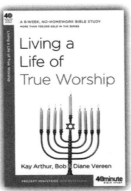

A 6-WEEK, NO-HOMEWORK BIBLE STUDY
MORE THAN 700,000 SOLD IN THE SERIES

Living a Life of True Worship

Kay Arthur, Bob & Diane Vereen

ABOUT THE AUTHORS AND
PRECEPT MINISTRIES INTERNATIONAL

KAY ARTHUR is known around the world as an international Bible teacher, author, conference speaker, and host of the national radio and television programs *Precepts for Life,* which reaches a worldwide viewing audience of over 94 million. A four-time Gold Medallion Award–winning author, Kay has authored more than 100 books and Bible studies.

Kay and her husband, Jack, founded Precept Ministries International in 1970 in Chattanooga, Tennessee, with a vision to establish people in God's Word. Today, the ministry has a worldwide outreach. In addition to inductive study training workshops and thousands of small-group studies across America, PMI reaches nearly 150 countries with inductive Bible studies translated into nearly 70 languages, teaching people to discover Truth for themselves.

GEORG HUBER has served as director of German-speaking Europe for Precept Ministries International since 1998. He leads Precept Upon Precept studies and conducts training workshops in inductive study throughout Europe in both German and English. A native of Vienna, Austria, Georg earned his doctorate from the University of Vienna. In addition to contributing to the 40-Minute Bible Studies series, he works as an editor and translator, making Precept materials available in the German language.

Contact Precept Ministries International for more information about inductive Bible studies in your area.

Precept Ministries International
P.O. Box 182218
Chattanooga, TN 37422-7218
800-763-8280
www.precept.org